Arts and Crafts
of the
AZTECS AND MAYA

Ting Morris

Illustrated by Emma Young

A⁺

Smart Apple Media

Published by Smart Apple Media
2140 Howard Drive West, North Mankato, MN 56003

Artwork by Emma Young
Designed by Helen James
Edited by Mary-Jane Wilkins
Picture research by Su Alexander

Photograph acknowledgements
page 5 Wolfgang Kaehler/Corbis; 6 Danny Lehman/Corbis; 7 Charles &
Josette Lenars/Corbis; 8 Free Agents Limited/Corbis; 9t Bettmann/Corbis,
b Craig Lovell/Corbis; 10 Morton Beebe/Corbis; 12 Charles & Josette
Lenars/Corbis; 13 Gianni Dagli Orti/Corbis; 14, 15 & 16 Werner Forman/
Corbis; 18 Burstein Collection/Corbis; 19t Kimbell Art Museum/Corbis,
b Danny Lehman/Corbis; 20 Charles & Josette Lenars/Corbis;
21 Bettmann/Corbis; 22 Danny Lehman/Corbis; 24 Charles & Josette
Lenars/Corbis; 25 Gianni Dagli Orti/Corbis; 26 Bohemian Nomad
Picturemakers/Corbis; 27 Archivo Iconografico, S.A./Corbis;
28 Wolfgang Kaehler/Corbis
Front cover: Werner Forman/Corbis

Printed in Singapore

Library of Congress Cataloging-in-Publication Data

Morris, Ting.
Aztecs and Maya / written by Ting Morris ; illustrated by Emma Young.
p. cm. — (Arts and crafts of the ancient world)
Includes index.
ISBN-13: 978-1-58340-915-2
1. Handicraft—Mexico—Juvenile literature. 2. Aztecs—Social life and
customs—Juvenile literature. 3. Mayas—Social life and customs—
Juvenile literature. 4. Mexico—History—To 1519—Juvenile
literature. I. Young, E. (Emma). II. Title. III. Series: Morris, Ting.
Arts and crafts of the ancient world.

TT28.M6M67 2006
680.972—dc22   2006002645

First Edition

9 8 7 6 5 4 3 2 1

Contents

9-11-07 $20.00

The world of the Aztecs and Maya

The Maya and the Aztecs were descendants of the earliest people who lived in Central America. The Maya built a powerful and successful civilization between A.D. 250 and 900. Mayan people spread across parts of the modern countries of Mexico, Guatemala, Belize, El Salvador, and Honduras.

The Aztecs came to power later. They were originally a tribe of wandering hunters from farther north, who moved south to the Valley of Mexico in the 12th century. Most Aztecs and Maya were farmers, and they lived in villages near their fields. Corn, beans, and squash were the most important crops. The Maya also built important cities and ceremonial centers, and the Aztec empire was run from their capital of Tenochtitlan. During the early 1500s, Spanish conquerors arrived in search of gold, and within a few years, they destroyed the Mayan and Aztec civilizations. Recently, archaeologists have recovered some of the things that were lost, including many wonderful works of art.

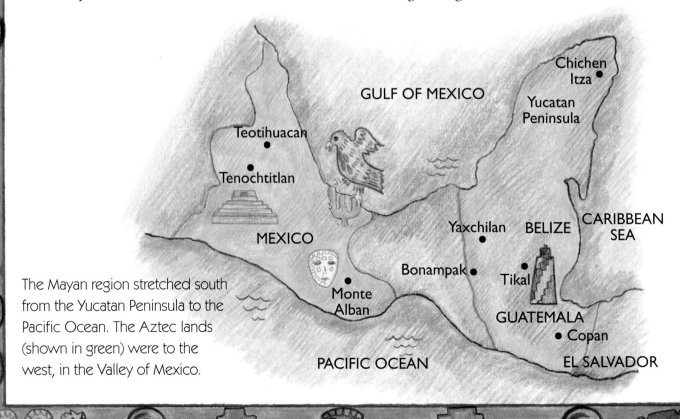

The Mayan region stretched south from the Yucatan Peninsula to the Pacific Ocean. The Aztec lands (shown in green) were to the west, in the Valley of Mexico.

This Mayan temple at Tikal, in Guatemala, is 154 feet (47 m) high. At the top of the central stairway is the entrance to a room where priests held rituals. In most of the rituals, the priests offered blood to the gods.

Pyramids and palaces

More than 2,000 years ago, the Maya started to build temples where they could worship their many gods. They made their temples in the shape of stepped pyramids. As the Mayan population grew, separate city-states developed. Each city had its own god-like ruler, who lived in a stone palace. He and his supporters controlled the surrounding villages and farmlands. After the Maya left their cities around A.D. 900, the cities fell into ruin and stayed untouched for many hundreds of years.

A New World

In 1519, a Spanish army led by Hernan Cortes arrived at the Aztec capital of Tenochtitlan. Two years later, after terrible battles and a long siege, the Spaniards captured the city and destroyed it. This was the end of the Aztec empire and the beginning of a new one for Europeans. They soon called this the New World, as people still do today. After destroying the Aztec capital, the conquerors built a new city on top of the ruins. This grew into Mexico City, one of the biggest cities in the world today.

Early stonework

The Maya and the Aztecs carried on traditions that had been started by earlier groups of people in Central America. We know little about these groups, but modern historians study stone monuments and other objects to learn more about their way of life.

The Olmecs were an early people who were the most successful from about 1200 to 400 B.C. They lived near the Gulf of Mexico, where they became skillful stoneworkers. The Olmecs carved small stone figures and an amazing series of giant stone heads. They carved the heads from huge boulders of a rock called basalt, which they must have dragged on sledges from mountains 60 miles (100 km) away. The largest stone head is 11 feet (3.4 m) high and may weigh 55 tons (50 t). Olmec craftsmen probably shaped the heads with stone tools.

A colossal Olmec stone head. Most experts believe that the heads are portraits of local rulers.

Temple carvings

The ancient city of Monte Alban sits on a mountaintop, overlooking the modern city of Oaxaca in southern Mexico. Monte Alban was the capital city of the Zapotecs, who first built it in about 500 B.C. One of the structures they built there is called the Temple of the Dancers. This building contains many stone slabs with carvings of strange male figures. Experts once thought these figures were dancing, but most now believe that they were the victims of war. Zapotec stoneworkers may have carved the slabs to mark the end of fighting with neighboring peoples.

Place of the gods

The city of Teotihuacan, to the northeast of modern Mexico City, began as a small settlement around 200 B.C. We know little about the people who lived there, but the ruined remains of the city tell us that they laid it out in a grid pattern. It was probably abandoned about A.D. 700 and was later found by the Aztecs, who gave it the name we use today.

A Zapotec carving. The craftsman probably first drew a sketch of the figure in charcoal on the flat stone. He then carved along the outlines.

Teotihuacan means "place of the gods." Its people were great stoneworkers, carving sculptures on and around their temples and other buildings. They are also famous for their stone masks, which they may have put in graves.

Mayan sculpture

From the earliest times, Mayan sculptors liked to work in relief. This meant carving figures or designs so that they stood out from a stone background. They originally painted the reliefs in bright colors, but today we can see only traces of the paint. Sculptors carved many monuments to honor Mayan rulers, and they were put up near palaces and temples.

The Maya also recorded dates and events on upright stone slabs, called stelae. Some showed portraits of a ruler at the front, with other details at the sides and back. Another sculpture was the chacmool, a figure with a stone bowl. This probably held the heart and blood of people who were sacrificed to the gods at temples.

Relief panels

The structures at the ancient Mayan city of Yaxchilan, in southern Mexico, are known as the Queen's Temple. Above the doorways are several limestone panels carved in relief. Lady Kabal Xook is in every one. She was the main wife of Shield Jaguar II, who ruled Yaxchilan

A chacmool figure lies before a pyramid temple at Chichen Itza.

from 681 to 742. The relief panels tell us a great deal about the rituals the Maya held at that time. They also show us what great artists the Maya were.

Power to the king

Archaeologists found nine relief-carved stelae at Copan, a Mayan city in Honduras. The stelae were dedicated to a king called 18 Rabbit, who ruled Copan at the same time as Shield Jaguar II led Yaxchilan. The king is surrounded by all kinds of ritual details, including a double-headed centipede. Most of the monuments stand in the open space of the Great Plaza at Copan, where they showed off the king's power and authority.

This panel shows the Yaxchilan ruler holding a flaming torch over his queen, who is pulling a cord through her tongue. This is to offer blood to the gods and help keep the world in balance.

Waxaklajuun Ubaah Kawiil (also known as 18 Rabbit) stares out from this magnificent stela at Copan. Some of his features have worn away over time.

Play the ball game

The Maya and the Aztecs played a sacred game on special ball courts at their ceremonial centers. The court was surrounded by high walls, and players tried to hit a solid rubber ball through a stone ring high on a wall. They hit the ball with their forearms, shoulders, elbows, and hips, but not with their hands. The game was an important ritual, and sometimes the losers were sacrificed to the gods.

Make a stone ring

You will need: modeling clay • cardboard • plaster of Paris • a rolling pin • a plastic mixing bowl • a stick • a round plastic bottle (11 inches, or 28 cm, in circumference) • a small plate (6–7 inches, or 15–18 cm) • a modeling tool • cooking oil • a lid • a fork • tape • a brush

A stone ring was the goal of the ball game. This one at Chichen Itza has carvings of two fighting snakes.

1 To make the round base, roll out a slab of modeling clay about three-quarters of an inch (2 cm) thick. Place a small plate on it as a guide and cut around it.

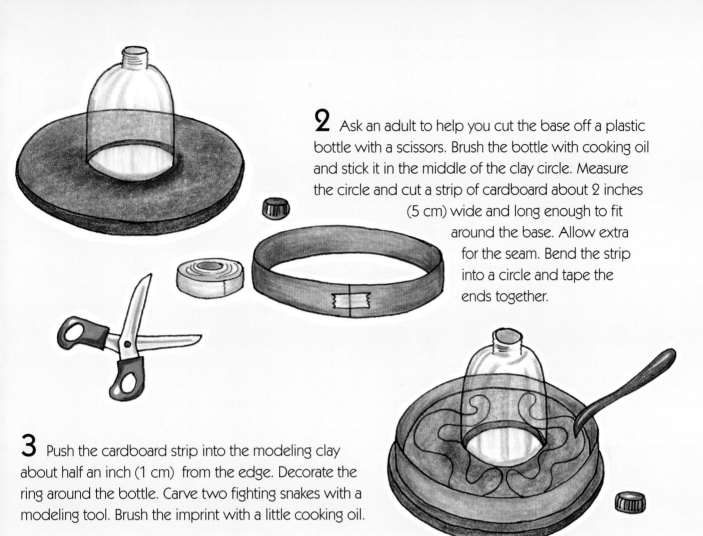

2 Ask an adult to help you cut the base off a plastic bottle with a scissors. Brush the bottle with cooking oil and stick it in the middle of the clay circle. Measure the circle and cut a strip of cardboard about 2 inches (5 cm) wide and long enough to fit around the base. Allow extra for the seam. Bend the strip into a circle and tape the ends together.

3 Push the cardboard strip into the modeling clay about half an inch (1 cm) from the edge. Decorate the ring around the bottle. Carve two fighting snakes with a modeling tool. Brush the imprint with a little cooking oil.

4 Mix 2 cups of plaster with 1 cup of water and stir well with a stick. Carefully pour the plaster into the ring, but don't fill the mold to the top. Important: never pour waste plaster down the sink! Press a pattern into the soft plaster with a lid and a fork. Lift the objects carefully to leave a clean impression in the plaster.

5 When the plaster is nearly dry, remove the cardboard rim and the bottle. When it has set hard, peel off the modeling clay. Smooth any rough edges with sandpaper.

Now you can play the ball game. See if you can hit a tennis ball through the ring without using your hands, head, or feet!

11

Aztec sculpture

Aztec craftsmen, including stoneworkers and sculptors, followed a great tradition in Central America. They used styles that survived from the Olmecs, Zapotecs, Teotihuacanos, and Maya, who all worked in stone.

The Aztecs probably also uncovered stonework from the past, just as modern archaeologists do. Historians believe that foreign artists lived in the Aztec capital, and they must have brought their own techniques. Most sculptors used tools made from a volcanic glass called obsidian, which was mined in the highlands of Mexico. They sharpened obsidian into knives, scrapers, and striking blades, and used sand and powdered rock to grind and shape stone surfaces.

Gods and goddesses

The Aztecs carved statues of their many gods and goddesses. People believed that the gods controlled the Aztec world. Sculptors mostly carved figures in relief, but some stone carvings are three-dimensional. Larger statues, such as the one of Xochipilli, were probably produced for temples or palaces. The god, who is more than three feet (1 m) high, sits on his own decorated altar.

These stone statues of standard-bearers were found at the bottom of a stairway at the Great Temple in Tenochtitlan (modern Mexico City).

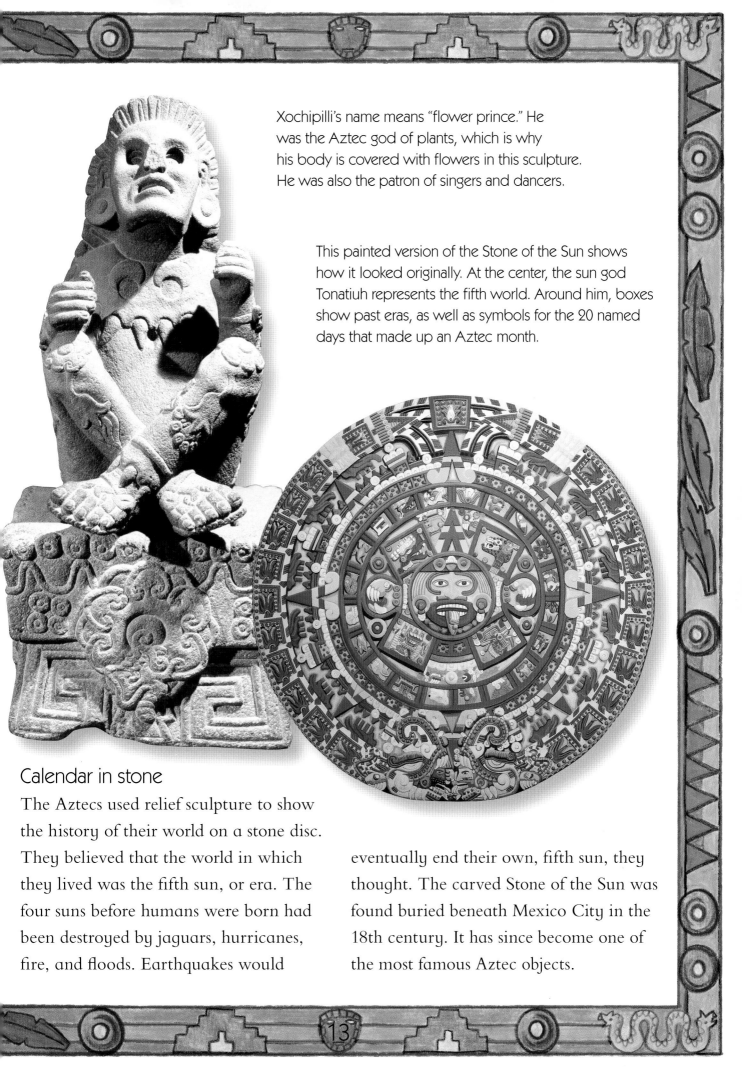

Xochipilli's name means "flower prince." He was the Aztec god of plants, which is why his body is covered with flowers in this sculpture. He was also the patron of singers and dancers.

This painted version of the Stone of the Sun shows how it looked originally. At the center, the sun god Tonatiuh represents the fifth world. Around him, boxes show past eras, as well as symbols for the 20 named days that made up an Aztec month.

Calendar in stone

The Aztecs used relief sculpture to show the history of their world on a stone disc. They believed that the world in which they lived was the fifth sun, or era. The four suns before humans were born had been destroyed by jaguars, hurricanes, fire, and floods. Earthquakes would eventually end their own, fifth sun, they thought. The carved Stone of the Sun was found buried beneath Mexico City in the 18th century. It has since become one of the most famous Aztec objects.

Precious metals and stones

The people of Central America valued precious metals and stones, as did other ancient civilizations around the world. One of the main reasons the Spanish invaded the region in the 16th century was to look for gold.

Spanish adventurers had heard tales of a king who ruled over a wealthy land and sprinkled gold dust on his skin every day. The Spaniards called him El Dorado, or the golden man, but they never found him or his land.

In fact, the Aztecs liked jade more than gold. The greatest workers in gold were the Mixtecs, who lived in central Mexico from about A.D. 900. They used gold, silver, jade, and turquoise to make small objects.

This gold pendant was made by a Mixtec craftsman. He may have sold it to the Aztecs.

This double-headed serpent from Tenochtitlan is made of turquoise. These fabulous creatures were symbols of the sky, and this ornament was probably worn by an Aztec priest.

Symbol of sun and corn

The Maya also admired jade, a hard stone made up of a mineral called jadeite, which can be different colors, ranging from green and gray to white and black. The Maya liked the bright green jade best, and they carved it into many shapes, including round beads. Mayan people put a jade bead in a dead person's mouth before burial, and the stone was used for masks placed on the face of dead rulers. This was probably because the Maya saw jade as a symbol of corn, their favorite food. The stone also represented the sun.

Turquoise

The stone called turquoise was very popular with the Toltecs, who came to power in the Mexican region around A.D. 900. They traded the greenish blue stone with the Aztecs. They brought it from the provinces of their empire to Tenochtitlan, where they cut and polished it into many wonderful objects. These included masks, shields, bracelets, and other pieces of jewelry.

Make a mosaic mask

The Aztecs and Maya decorated their shields, knife handles, and other objects with mosaic patterns. A mosaic is a design made up of small pieces of colored stone and other materials.

This Aztec mask is made of wood covered with small pieces of turquoise. The teeth and eyes are made of shell. It was probably worn by priests for special dances or rituals.

Make a mask

You will need: a round balloon and string • a pencil • glue • old newspaper • thin white cardboard • brushes • brown, black, and white poster paints • blue, green, turquoise, and red paper • scissors • petroleum jelly • masking tape

1 Blow up the balloon until it is a bit bigger than your head. Tie it firmly with string and coat it with a thin layer of petroleum jelly. Tear newspaper into one-inch-wide (2.5 cm) strips. Pour glue into a bowl and dilute it with about the same amount of water, to the consistency of thin cream.

2 Cover the balloon with a layer of paper. Coat the pieces with glue on both sides and stick them on. Hold the balloon in place on top of a bowl. For the second layer, mix a little paint into the adhesive so you can see the difference between the layers. Build up five or six layers in this way. Leave to dry for at least 24 hours.

3 When the paper layers are dry, draw a line to mark the mask shape around the balloon and cut it out. Peel away the balloon. Mark the position of your eyes and cut small eye holes. To make a nose, cut a cardboard triangle and fold it in half. Stick it on with masking tape.

4 Paint the mask brown to look like wood and leave to dry. Meanwhile, cut mosaic shapes from the colored paper. Stick the paper pieces to the dry mask one by one with glue. Cover it completely with mosaic patterns, except for the eyes and a big mouth.

5 Paint the eyes with white and black poster paint. Cut out a red paper mouth and white cardboard teeth and glue them onto the mask. When dry, varnish the mask with a thin coat of glue. If you want to wear it, make holes in the sides and thread ribbon through. Tie on the mask and amaze your friends.

Clay and pottery

The Maya and the Aztecs used clay to make vessels and many other objects, including figurines, incense burners, and whistles. Craftsmen made them all by hand. The potter's wheel was introduced later by Europeans.

This Mayan earthenware plate shows the range of colors potters produced, from creamy yellow to red and black.

The Maya and Aztecs rolled their clay into coils and put them together to build up a pot or similar object. They used wet clay to stick the coils together and then smoothed the shape when it was complete. Sometimes they pounded the clay into flat slabs and fitted these together. They decorated their creations with carvings or paint and baked them in simple kilns. Finally, they painted them with a mixture of clay and water called slip.

Telling a story

After about A.D. 700, Mayan artists carved clay vessels in relief. Many of the carvings were based on myths and legends. A favorite myth was the story of the Hero Twins, who the Maya believed were the first people of the present world. They were challenged to play the sacred ball game by the Lords of the Underworld and on their way to the ball court had to pass various tests. The heroes eventually won the ball game and sentenced the Lords of the Underworld to become servants, grinding corn and making pots for humans.

This carved clay vessel was made around 750. The carving shows one of the Hero Twins holding an ax to fight off a monster.

Warrior guardians

We know from some finds that the Aztecs made life-sized statues from clay. The large statues were made in separate pieces and then put together. At the Great Temple in Mexico City, archaeologists discovered two statues that guarded the entrance to the main room. They were eagle warriors, who made up one of the two great military societies, along with jaguar warriors. The clay eagle warrior has become a famous Aztec object.

This clay eagle warrior was made about 1450. He wears the feathers of a giant eagle, and his helmet is shaped like the bird's open beak.

Writing and books

The Maya developed their own system of writing. It was based on a large number of symbols, called pictographs or glyphs. Some symbols stood for whole words, while others were sounds or parts of words.

This relief sculpture from the Mayan city of Tikal, in Guatemala, shows carved glyphs.

Mayan scribes were important and were probably the only people, apart from the rulers, priests, and nobles, who could read the glyphs. The scribes carved important dates and events on walls and stone slabs. They also used quills made from turkey feathers to write on fig tree bark. They sometimes wrote on one long strip of bark, then folded it in an accordion shape to make the pages of a book.

Aztec books

Later, the Aztecs made books in the same way; we call these folded books codices (the plural of codex). Unfortunately, the Spanish conquerors destroyed many of these books, and very few codices still exist today.

Codex Mendoza

The Aztec book called the Codex Mendoza was written and painted just after the Spanish invasion. It was made by the first Spanish viceroy in Mexico and sent to the King of Spain. The book is kept in a library at Oxford University. It has 71 pages and several sections. One goes through the years from the founding of Tenochtitlan in 1325 to its destruction in 1521. The first page of the Codex Mendoza shows the founding of the Aztec capital. According to legend, the Aztecs settled where they found an eagle perched on a cactus. A Spanish priest who knew the Aztec language wrote explanations on some of the pictures.

From Mexico to Madrid

One of the four existing Mayan codices is called the Madrid Codex, because that is where it is kept. It has 112 pages and has sections about rain ceremonies, planting and farming, new year, deer hunting, and trapping, as well as capturing and sacrificing prisoners. Experts are not sure when the codex was written, but most believe it was during the 15th or 16th century. It was then taken to Spain and was only rediscovered in the 19th century.

These pages from the Madrid Codex show sacrifices being made to bring rain. Snakes weave their way across the pages. The picture symbols represent the 260 days of the sacred calendar.

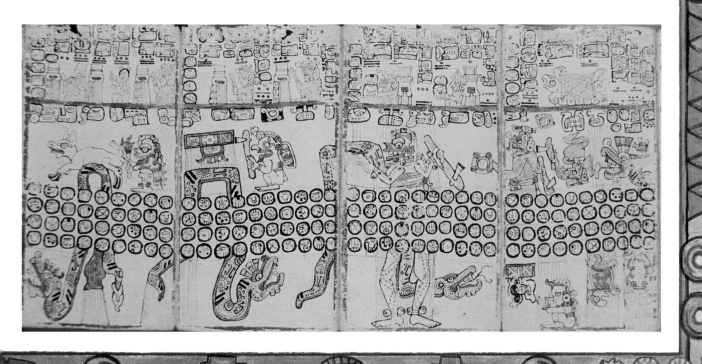

Make a paper cutout

The Maya made paper by putting fig tree bark in water and pounding the fibers until they were like cloth. The sheets were then dried in the sun and given a thin coating of lime to make a smooth surface for writing and painting. Some Native Americans from Mexico, such as the Otomi people, carry on the tradition of painting and cutting bark paper today. The Otomi fold sheets of homemade bark paper in half and cut out symmetrical figures. These paper spirits are said to bring good or bad luck.

This painting was made on homemade bark paper by an Otomi artist in modern Mexico.

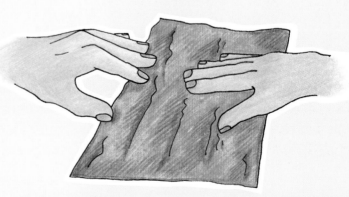

Make paper cutouts

You will need: brown wrapping paper
• a pencil • scissors

1 Making bark paper is difficult, but here's a way of making brown paper look like an Otomi sheet. Cut two 8- by 10-inch (20 x 25 cm) paper rectangles and crumple each into a ball. Then flatten out the paper and smooth it with your hand. Crumple and flatten the sheets three or four times until the paper is soft and smooth.

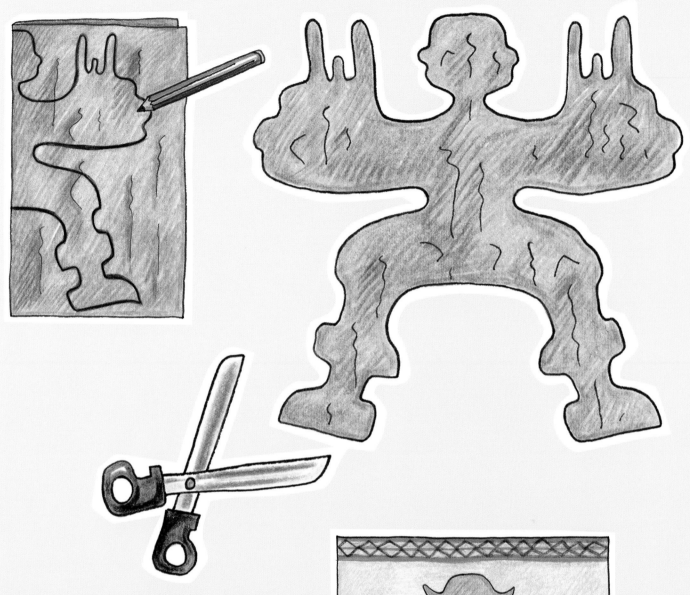

2 Fold the paper in half lengthwise and draw half a person or animal against the folded edge. Make up your own magic figure or copy this paper spirit. Trace the pattern (you can make it larger on a photocopier), cut it out, and fold it in half. Then place it on the paper and draw around it.

3 Cut around the outline and open the paper. Now make the other cutout in the same way. Stick one paper spirit on a card and give it to someone as a present. Keep the other one—it might bring you good luck!

Maya and Aztec painting

The Maya and the Aztecs painted the stonework of buildings, as well as their relief sculptures, figurines, and pottery. Smooth, plastered walls made the best surfaces for painting, and we know that Mayan artists painted early tombs in cream, red, and black.

In 1989, archaeologists working at the ancient city of Copan, in Honduras, discovered a shrine inside a larger, later temple. The shrine was built around A.D. 570 by Moon Jaguar, king of Copan. It was painted mainly in red, the color that stood for blood and life for the Maya. There were also shades of green and yellow. Red was the most popular color with artists who decorated pottery.

This fresco from Room 1 at Bonampak shows masked actors at a procession.

The walls of Bonampak

In 1946, explorers in southern Mexico found a Mayan building at a place they named Bonampak (meaning "painted walls"). They gave it that name because they discovered that three rooms of the palace were covered with brilliant frescoes. These had been painted on damp plaster around 790.

The first room had paintings of a magnificent procession. Room 2 showed battle scenes. And in the third room were pictures of a ceremonial dance and ritual bloodletting. Many of the paintings have brilliant blue backgrounds. The Maya made this color from a mineral called azurite, which they found near copper deposits. They ground the blue mineral into a powder and mixed it with water to make the paint.

Aztec temples

The Aztecs also painted their pyramids, temples, and palaces. The Great Temple at Tenochtitlan was painted in bright colors. Artists brushed the paint onto a layer of plaster that covered the cut stone slabs of the pyramid temple. At the top of the pyramid were two shrines. One shrine was dedicated to Huitzilopochtli, the god of the sun and war and the city's patron, and was painted red. The other shrine, built in honor of Tlaloc, the god of rain, was blue.

This modern illustration shows Aztec artists drawing and painting on bark paper and plastered walls. The Aztecs made their colors from ground minerals and plants.

Baskets, textiles, and feathers

The Maya region was full of materials needed for many crafts. Traditional techniques were passed on through the generations, and visitors to Mexico and Central America can still see the results in street markets and craft shops today.

This modern Mexican craft shop displays baskets made in the traditional way.

A large central market in the Aztec capital sold baskets of all shapes and sizes. They were used for storing corn and other foods, as well as for carrying produce home or to market. Basket makers wove, twined, and braided the stalks of various reeds that grew beside lakes. They also used the stalks and leaves of the Mexican agave plant. Reeds were used to make floor mats. These were important to people who had little furniture in their homes.

Mayan textiles

Mayan women made clothes for their families. They wove fibers from the agave plant for tough clothing and used cotton for more comfortable clothes or outfits for special occasions. They made the textiles on a simple loom made of sticks, rope, and a strap. The weaver wore the strap around her waist and could set up the loom anywhere. Mayan women could work indoors or outside, and they sometimes gathered in a building that was set aside for weaving. They produced mainly geometric designs, and these are still popular with people in southern Mexico and Guatemala today.

Featherwork

Aztec featherworkers wove, tied, or glued the stems of feathers into fabric. They used great skill to make feathered headdresses, ceremonial shields, cloaks, and fans. Their huntsmen gathered the feathers by netting birds in the tropical forests. Some colorful birds were also kept in cages for the same purpose.

This portrait shows the Aztec emperor Montezuma II carrying a magnificent feathered shield. Montezuma was emperor at the time of the Spanish invasion.

Make a feather headdress

Today, many Mexican people celebrate their Aztec past at special festivals. They dress up in traditional Aztec costumes and wear bright feathers.

This drummer wears a homemade headdress at an Aztec festival.

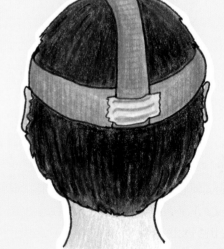

Make an Aztec headdress

You will need: corrugated cardboard • straws • red, blue, green, yellow, and white tissue paper • strong glue • packaging tape • a thick black felt pen

1 Cut a strip of cardboard about 22 inches (56 cm) long and 2 inches (5 cm) wide. Ask a friend to fit it around your head and stick the ends together with packaging tape. Attach another strip to the center back and bring the loose end over the crown of the head. Attach it at the front so that it sits comfortably. Tape it firmly.

2 Crunch large pieces of blue tissue paper into walnut-sized balls. Tear some yellow and green tissue paper into small pieces and crunch them into marble-sized pieces. Glue the decorations to the outside of the headband.

3 Draw feather outlines, about 8 inches (20 cm) long, on tissue paper. Cut out red, blue, and white feathers. Draw markings on the white feathers with a felt pen.

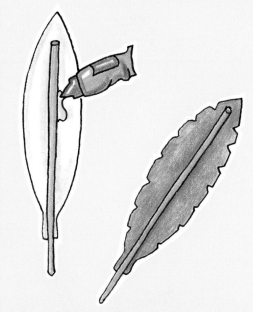

4 Stick the straws onto the feathers, leaving about one and a half inches (4 cm) of each straw sticking out at the bottom. Make a few small feathers with shorter straws. Then, fringe the feathers.

5 Push the ends of the straws into the holes of the cardboard headband. Arrange the feathers in a pattern and push some in from the bottom. Put on the headdress and make another one for your friend.

Glossary

altar A flat-topped structure where religious ceremonies are performed.

archaeologist A person who studies the ancient past by digging up and looking at remains.

azurite A deep blue mineral.

basalt A dark volcanic kind of rock.

ceremonial Having to do with ceremonies, especially important religious or public events (which took place at a ceremonial center).

chacmool A reclining stone figure with a bowl on its lap.

charcoal A black form of carbon made by heating wood.

city-state An independent state made up of a city and surrounding land.

codex (plural codices) A collection of texts in the form of a book.

commemorate To honor the memory of something or someone.

deity A god or goddess.

earthenware Clay pottery that has to be glazed to become waterproof.

era A very long period of time.

figurine A small figure or statuette.

fresco A wall painting made on damp plaster.

glyph A symbol (or pictograph) used in the writing system of hieroglyphics.

incense A fragrant gum.

kiln An oven used for firing, or baking, clay pots.

loom A device for weaving thread into cloth.

mineral A solid chemical substance that occurs naturally in the earth.

mosaic The art of making a picture or design with small pieces of colored material such as stone. The picture is also called a mosaic.

obsidian A hard, glassy volcanic rock.

patron The special guardian of a group of people.

pendant An ornament hanging from a piece of jewelry, or a piece of jewelry with ornaments hanging from it.

provinces The outer regions of an empire or a kingdom.

relief A sculpture in which figures or designs stand out from the background.

ritual A series of religious ceremonies or acts.

sacrifice To kill a person or an animal as an offering to a god.

scribe A person who writes out documents.

shrine A sacred place of worship.

siege A military operation in which an army surrounds a place and forces the people there to surrender.

slip A mixture of clay and water applied by potters.

stela (plural stelae) An upright stone slab with an inscription.

vessel A hollow container, especially for holding liquids.

Zapotecs An ancient people of southern Mexico.

Index